INTRODUCTION + WELCOME

Hello!

We are excited and honored you went looking for a workbook on launching your private practice! This workbook is packed with logistics, important information, and it's designed to empower you every step of the way! Becoming a business owner as a therapist is full of uncharted territory and unknowns. This workbook aims to shed light on everything you need to know before or during your business launch. Inspired by our lived experience as mental health leaders, which birthed courses we've taught to graduate level counselors-in-training over the years, this workbook serves as a guide to check out all domains of self that are necessary for building and sustaining a nourishing and social-justice-informed private practice. Here's to the journey that stretches us personally and professionally, let's jump in!

In getting started, here are some reminders we hope you will carry with you through this workbook.

- We need us all for this work, we are so glad you are here.

- Please take care + breaks as needed. Building a business takes time.

- We are humans existing in this moment in time, and that is intense, *more on this below*.

- Move as you need and want. Bodies have a lot of information, go to the body when feeling stuck.

- Trust the process. We have a plan, it is here in the workbook and trust that you are where you should be and wherever this takes you.

- We won't cover it all, there is not just one way and this is just the beginning.

- Experiment knowing many things will not work out.

- WELCOME :)

Why a Sustainable Private Practice?

Sustainability Defined per *Oxford Languages* Dictionary:

sus·tain·a·bil·i·ty
/səˌstānəˈbilədē/

noun

    able to be maintained at a certain rate or level.
    able to be upheld or defended.
    ability to continue over a long period of time.

We are humans existing in this moment in time, and that existence can feel intense. The world around us is complex, ever-changing, and often heavy — and our work as therapists, healers, and helpers is deeply intertwined with the current reality. Therapy has always reflected the world we live in. Whether or not we name it, therapy is shaped by culture, by current events, and by the conditions in which we and our clients live.

There are so many days when we sit in our offices as therapists and our clients discuss the ways the world is not designed for them, and the impact that has on their mental health. Our job as therapists is often validating, supporting, and creating space for all the feelings. We also believe that our job is to support clients moving forward AND to create a better world. It's WHY we believe that creating a business with sustainability at its core is essential.

Building a private practice is not just about managing a business; it's about creating a life and livelihood that reflect your values. A sustainable and nourishing practice means one that supports you as much as it supports your clients. It means building rhythms, systems, and boundaries that make the work sustainable — financially, emotionally, and energetically — over time.

This kind of practice asks us to slow down, to be intentional, and to understand the broader forces that shape our work: capitalism, perfectionism, productivity culture, burnout, and scarcity. Recognizing these patterns allows us to imagine and build something different — something grounded in care, reciprocity, and sustainability.

We believe that by designing practices that are nourishing, spacious, and rooted in integrity, we create ripple effects beyond ourselves. A sustainable practice models a different way of being in relationship with work — one that honors rest, interdependence, equity, and community.

By building a business with sustainability at its core, we believe you can create an example of a different more sustainable way of existing. We believe that to build a socially justice centered business you need to understand the ways that white supremacy, capitalism, racism, sexism, and ableism, impact you and your work. We hope this workbook is a starting place. We also believe that building a business with collaboration, equitable pay, accessible spaces, and self-care at the core will enable you to be a business owner that can change the world.

We're so glad you're here.

TABLE OF CONTENTS

Structure of this Workbook

Each section will have an introduction and overview of each exercise followed by a final tip on how to keep sustainability in mind. Additionally, each exercise will have a quote or piece of advice from other therapists in community to highlight that we are not alone in this work. As authors, we recognize our own perspective and don't want to be the only voices present throughout this book. That's why we've included additional voices, contacts, and strategies in hopes of deepening the work.

EXERCISE 1

To Begin: A Grounding Exercise

As you read in our introduction, this workbook is to help you mentally and logistically prepare for launching a sustainable private practice as a mental health professional. Let's start with a grounding exercise to support you being present as we begin.

Welcome, you have already begun and let's take a moment to ground and pause. Find a comfortable position—sitting with your feet on the ground, standing tall, or lying down if that feels right. Gently close your eyes or have a soft gaze down.

Take a slow, deep breath in through your nose, and exhale fully through your mouth. Take a moment to notice what you hear and feel. Acknowledge and honor all it took for you to get to this moment.

On your next inhale and exhale, take a moment to imagine putting your to-do list aside. Knowing we are all coming from something and going somewhere, and in this moment you are here.

When you are ready we will offer a few phrases, just notice what comes up for you:

- You are not alone in this work and we need you for this work

- You are capable of creating a business that is nourishing and sustainable and rooted in social justice

- You will not know it all, this is just the beginning and there will be time.

Inhale deeply one more time, exhale slowly, and when you feel ready, open your eyes. Bring this grounded sense of presence with you as we move into the workbook.

SPEAKING TO SUSTAINABILITY

When we support ourselves with grounding, we allow ourselves to operate from a place that is calm, and supported. When we move from a place that is not grounded, we often make mistakes or decisions that are not informed or in our best interest. When we can ground and be in our nervous system, we can make decisions that will sustain us and our practice.

"To be maintained at a certain level" is one definition of sustainability. Perhaps grounding can support a steady rhythm by coming to business decisions from a rooted, calm place. How else can you remain grounded throughout this workbook? How can your five senses (see, taste, touch, hear, smell) help you?

A private practice can take thoughtfulness, patience, and creativity to build. Think outside the box with where and how you advertise, what programs and events you participate in, and any paid services you choose to use. Your caseload may build quickly or slowly, but it's going to take dedication and a lot of effort. You can absolutely do this, just believe in yourself and take action. I met the Groupon person at a women's networking event, and sparked her interest in running a Groupon for an art therapy session at a low cost. This filled my caseload and started a word-of-mouth referral base, and I never had to make major marketing efforts after that. But as an introvert, I almost didn't go to that networking event. I nearly missed this great opportunity!

—Kate King, MA. LPC. ATR-BC, The Radiant Life Project

EXERCISE 2

Finding Your Why

Before you begin with the logistics, and after you ground yourself, allow yourself to dream. Why did you open this workbook? What brought you here? Take 10 or more minutes to imagine what your private practice could be and do, for you, for your community, for the world. We invite you to write, reflect, or do art with the following prompts:

- Think about what you would hope the work feels like?
- What does it look like? Sound like?
- What would your schedule be like?
- What would the work environment be like?
- What would you wear to work?
- How would you feel at work and when you are not at work?
- What are your hopes, dreams, and aspirations about private practice?
- What are your concerns and fears?
- How will you integrate self-care into your private practice and/or in your role as a therapist?

SPEAKING TO SUSTAINABILITY

Give yourself the space to dream and imagine what could be. This is the time to be creative and let that support your business plan. When we start with our WHY it becomes the thing we can return to, sustaining us in this work. It can of course evolve as you evolve, so give yourself a starting place.

Build a practice based on your values, not the values of what other therapists say to build it on. If you're going to go all-in on owning your own business, make sure you feel aligned with the mission and values so you can one step at a time figure out what your next right move is.

—Stephanie Konter-O'Hara, LPC, Owner at WellMinded Counseling in Colorado

EXERCISE 3

Building Your Business Roadmap

Craving some structure in all the possibilities of private practice? Here's a checklist to consider when starting up your business! Please feel free to make a copy of this checklist to revisit as needed during your business growth.

- ☐ **1**   Get Grounded + Find Your Why
- ☐ **2**   Build and Protect Your Self-Care Plan
- ☐ **3**   Naming Exercise and Pick a Name
- ☐ **4**   Build Your Budget and Choose Your Business Entity
- ☐ **5**   Get an EIN
- ☐ **6**   Get an NPI
- ☐ **7**   Open a Bank Account
- ☐ **8**   Get Insurance
- ☐ **9**   Choose HIPAA Compliant Software
- ☐ **10**   Set Up Your Bookkeeping System
- ☐ **11**   Begin Marketing Authentically
- ☐ **12**   Plan How You'll File Taxes
- ☐ **13**   Live in the Joy of Both/And Beyond

Get Grounded + Find Your Why: A starting place in rooting you in your values, be sure to go back to Exercise 1+2: Your Aspirations to spend some time discovering your purpose and vision of private practice.

Build and Protect Your Self-Care Plan: The cornerstone of sustainability as a small business owner and therapist, check out Exercise 4: Self-Care & Private Practice, Exercise 15: Burnout & Systemic Issues and Exercise 18: Sustainable Urgency and Work-Life Harmony.

Naming Exercise and Pick a Name: One fun and creative example of being in business, check out Exercise 7: Name Your Business.

Build Your Budget and Choose Your Business Entity: The left-side logic of the business world, engage in Exercise 9: Know Your Numbers: Budgeting in Private Practice.

Get an EIN: This will cost you nothing, so beware of scams! Make sure you are on the .gov website. Once you apply for an EIN, which is often described as the Social Security Number of your business, you'll get an email usually within 5-10 minutes with the number, structured as XX-XXXXXXX. Make sure to store it in a safe and easy-access place! Additionally, you'll want to register your business with your state government website.

Get an NPI: A unique identifier for your work as a therapist, you may already have an NPI for you as an individual. Now you'll go to the NPPES website to get an organizational NPI, which is also free and takes a few minutes to complete.

Open a Bank Account: Do your research on which bank or credit union meets your needs. Do you need Bill Pay? Zelle? Easy transfers between accounts? Does the account have a fee attached to it? Do you need a business credit card or savings account in addition to a business checking account?

Get Insurance: Not all insurances are created equal. Speak to a mental health lawyer or poll colleagues on which malpractice/liability insurance they have and why.

Choose HIPAA Compliant Software: There are comparison videos out there on the internet to see what you get for your monthly fee. Do you want telehealth built in? Automatic reminders? Payment integration? The more features, the higher the fee. You can also ask colleagues which one they use and why.

Set Up Your Bookkeeping System: This is critical. Your Electronic Health Record (EHR) is NOT accounting software. So where will you keep records for your business? Quickbooks is expensive but has lovely reports, Wave is the cheaper version. You can also consider an Excel or Google Sheet to track payments if wanting to keep costs low. Other folks will delegate this to a bookkeeping professional for peace of mind. Explore the questions to ask this type of professional with Exercise 14: Selecting Supports.

Begin Marketing Authentically: This could be a course or workbook all in itself! Be sure to complete Exercise 11: PsychologyToday Bingo and Your Website Copy, Exercise 12: Identifying Your Ideal Client, and Exercise 13: Elevator Pitch Practice

Plan How You'll File Taxes: Another example of when a do-it-yourself approach could be risky, we encourage you to find a tax professional well-versed in private practice. Review the questions to ask with Exercise 14: Selecting Supports.

Live in the Joy of Both/And Beyond: Building and maintaining a business isn't for the faint of heart. Be sure to revisit your Why often, as well as complete Exercise 19: Interviewing Your Community and Exercise 20: Letter from Your Future Private Practice Self in order to remain rooted in your purpose and vision.

SPEAKING TO SUSTAINABILITY

We love a good checklist for accountability! What would you add? How can you come back to the checklist to ensure you are on track? A checklist keeps you focused and reduces overwhelm.

1. Your growth as a therapist is nonlinear. Expect spirals, ruptures, twists and turns. 2. Let your practice truly reflect you and learn about how to market the skills you already have! 3. Go to therapy and/or do your own personal work in a meaningful way. 4. Be flexible. Move between modalities and approaches based on what the client's nervous system needs. 5. Seek consistent/ethical consultation with other therapists. Working in a siloed way can be harmful to you and your clients. 6. Practice humility and curiosity. True expertise comes from ongoing learning, self-awareness, and integrating new knowledge over time.

—Morgen Villegas, LCSW, LAC (she/her) Vida Idilica Therapy and Consulting

EXERCISE 4

Self-Care & Private Practice

Caring for myself is not self-indulgence, it is self-preservation and that is an act of political warfare.

—Audre Lorde

Self-care means taking time to do things that help you feel well and support your physical and mental health. For your mental health, self-care can help you handle stress, lower your risk of getting sick, and boost your energy. Even small acts of self-care each day can make a big difference.

Self-care looks different for everyone, so it's important to find what works and feels good for you. It might take some trial and error to figure out what helps most. While self-care is not a cure for mental illness, knowing what triggers your symptoms and which coping skills help you can make a difference.

The World Health Organization defines self-care as: *"the ability of individuals, families, and communities to promote health, prevent disease, maintain health, and to cope with illness and disability with or without the support of a healthcare provider."*

Self-care can include physical, mental, emotional, and spiritual care.

Much of the research and conversation about self-care comes from a Western perspective, especially in the United States. I (Sam) think a lot of this culture is shaped by Western ideas, and I want to point that out. I'd like to share a short history because knowing where self-care comes from helps us see how broad it can be. Self-care started as a way to make care more inclusive, part of daily life, and easier to access.

Understanding self-care and how you practice it is important. It sets the foundation for how you show up as a therapist and business owner. We start here because, without a self-care plan, it's very hard to build a successful or sustainable business.

WHAT IS SELF-CARE? AN ORIGIN STORY

1950s

It was coined to describe activities that allowed institutionalized patients to preserve some physical independence—simple tasks that helped nurture a sense of self-worth, such as exercising and personal grooming.

1960s

Academics began taking a serious interest in post-traumatic stress disorder in first responders.

1970s

The concept of self-care really took off in North America, when the Black Panther Party began promoting it as essential for all Black citizens, as a means of staying resilient while experiencing the repeated injuries of systemic, interpersonal and medical racism.

1980s

Women's rights activists were inspired by groups such as the Black Panthers and began adapting their own ideas of what self-care meant for women, namely those living in poverty without access to healthcare. Ignored and often criticized by the government for their need for healthcare such as reproductive services, feminist activists opened their own health clinics to ensure that women were given access to the care that they needed. It is infuriating to realize that access to these basic rights is still labeled an act of rebellion. The late activist Audre Lorde wrote the now-famous quote, "Caring for myself is not self-indulgence, it is self-preservation, and that is an act of political warfare."

2000s

After the 9/11 terrorist attacks, the concept of self-care began rising again.

2020+

Yet again after President Donald Trump got elected.

Many Americans now practice self-care, but Sarah Mirk of Bitch Media writes that many ignore the "race, gender, and class dynamics behind the concept." People of color and women experience higher levels of stress than other members of the population, so it is necessary for these groups to take care of themselves.

Self-care has in many ways been turned into an industry far from its roots.

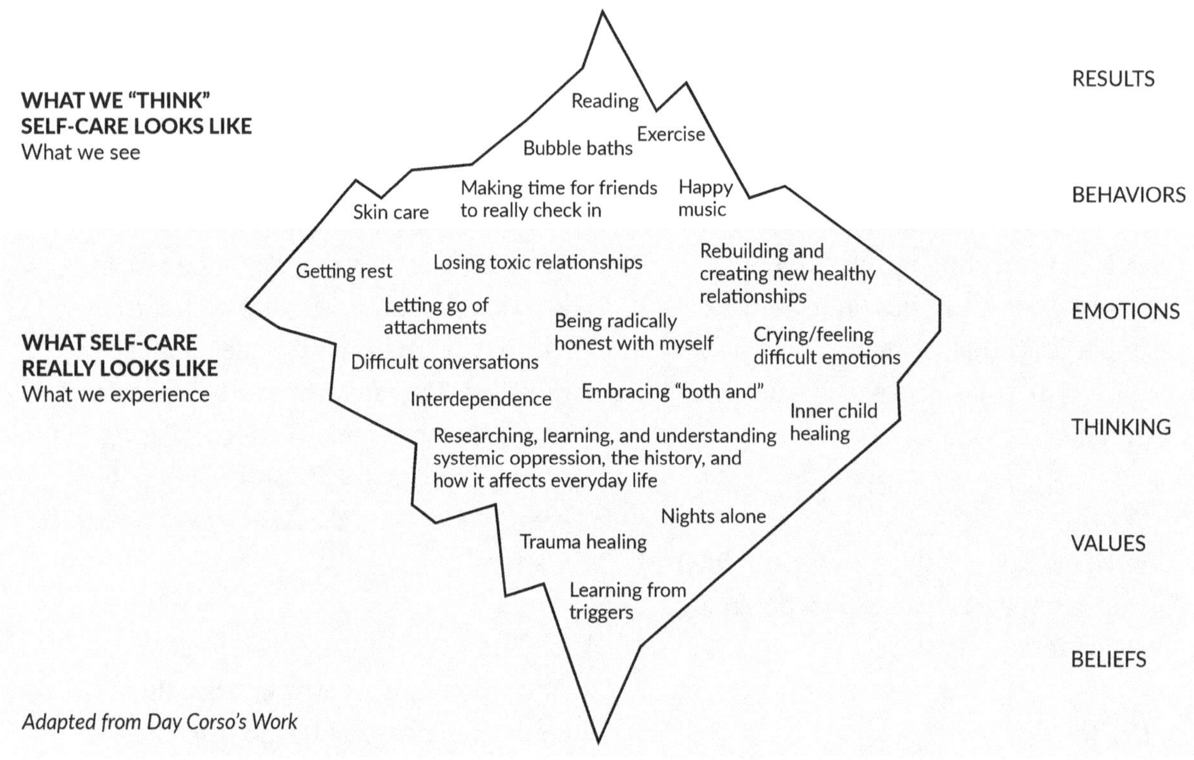

TAKE CARE EXERCISES

The exercises that follow are to support you if you are feeling stuck. They are a starting place.

Self-Care Checklist

Use the checklist as a starting place.

- Have you had enough/or any sleep?
- Water?
- Nourishment?

- Movement?
- Outside time?
- Start here if you feel stuck.

Self-Care Plan

For the self-care plan, brainstorm go-to people, places and things you can do to support yourself. This is something we encourage you to keep working on and to keep nearby. What can you do for your physical self-care? What can you do for your mental self-care? Your emotional self-care and who are your go-to supportive people? There can be some overlap let's see what you come up with.

MY SELF-CARE CHECKLIST
Have you done the following today...

If you are feeling stuck, start with this self-care checklist. Are any of the following present for you now? If your answer is no, start with one category to see if tending to yourself can support you moving forward.

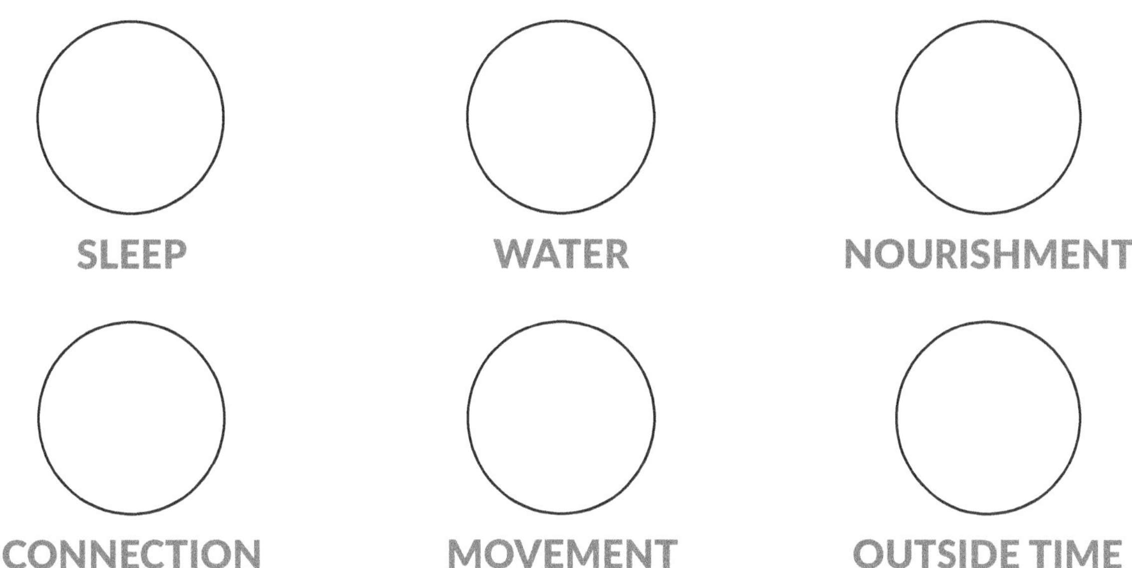

MY SELF-CARE PLAN

Fill in these bubbles with what you can do to take care of your physical, mental, or emotional self. When you don't know where to start taking on care, you can start here. Also fill in the bubble for supportive people in your life. This becomes a cheat sheet for when you are struggling. Let this exercise be your guide.

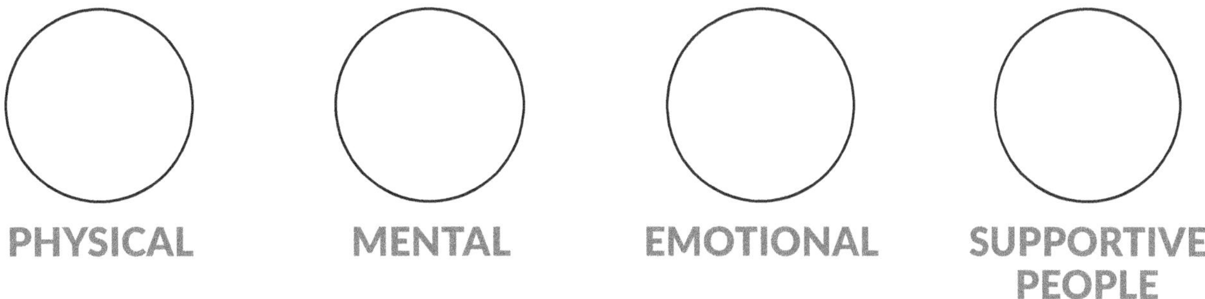

TAKE CARE CHECK-IN

The Take Care Check-in was designed by Michelle Castor and can be used as a brainstorming tool.

1 What are some of the ways I know that it might be time to take care?

2 What are some strategies I can do? Short-term? Long-term?

3 How can I tell I am stressed, activated, or triggered?

4 In the moment, I can...

Adapted in collaboration with Agua y Sangre, Michelle Castor

SPEAKING TO SUSTAINABILITY

As you have read, self-care is a buzzword, so we encourage you to pick your own word as you think about this concept. How can self-care be placed on your calendar amidst working ON your business (i.e. admin or marketing) and working IN your business (i.e. client work)? There is no sustainable business without self-care. Allow yourself the time and space for self-care, don't wait for the 'right' time. Additionally, we know self-care is now an overused word and industry, so pick a word that resonates most to you! How would you describe the practice of taking care in order to support yourself and your business?

Do not give up on yourself. Just as healing is not linear, this journey too does not follow a straight path. Don't let imposter syndrome win. Remember you did all the work to get you where you are! Keep at it and give yourself time to enjoy life in the process. As we advise, self-care is a must!

—Arely Garcia, LCSW

EXERCISE 5

Pros/Cons of Private Practice

Let's try a word association exercise. Fill in the blank:

Private Practice is ________________________________.

Private Practice is ________________________________.

Private Practice is ________________________________.

Private Practice is ________________________________.

What's the overall vibe of your answers? Are you excited and can't wait to get started? Is there a part of you worrying about the effort it will take to run your own business? All parts are welcome!

As you consider if private practice is a fit for your personal and professional goals, what do you see as the pros and cons? Write some positives or 'pros' on the lines below. What about challenges or 'cons'? Once you've flushed out each list, ask colleagues in private practice to share their thoughts. What would they add?

Finally, as you review all the pros in that particular list, assign a percentage of weight or importance to each item adding up to 100%. For example, how important is it to you to have a flexible schedule? 50% Higher income? 30% The ability to have Fridays off? 20%

Do the same percentages practice on the cons list. Highlight the highest percentage item on each list. What stands out to you? What are you noticing about the weighted/most important items?

	Positives/Pros	**Challenges/Cons**
Example	*A flexible schedule 50%*	*Finding clients 45%*

SPEAKING TO SUSTAINABILITY

How is sustainability reflected in your list of pros and cons? What items could be added to the list when keeping sustainability in mind?

Forget the myth that the grass is going to be greener on the private practice side of the lawn. That mindset is a trap. The truth is, the grass is green where you maximize your strengths and mitigate your weaknesses. Maybe that's doing private practice. Maybe not. It's not enough to be a gifted therapist; you must also be a grounded entrepreneur. Thriving is about finding the right shade of green for you in your space on the lawn and cheering on others on the lawn who have found their space and shade of green too.

—Ashley Jordan, LICSW Perspective Counseling, Auburn AL, 12 years in private practice

EXERCISE 6

Ten Principles of Private Practice

We created the Ten Principles as a way to highlight the logistical steps to take when building a private practice and we wanted to offer principles to keep in mind, as a way of saying it is not just what you do but how you do it. Check these out to see what resonates with you.

SPEAKING TO SUSTAINABILITY

This work is about process not just product. Which principles resonate with you? Why? Why not? What would it look like for you to write your own principles?

Have patience and trust the process. It's a journey to find your niche, your administrative systems, and your schedule. You gotta just start where you can and start meeting your needs. You'll find your authenticity and what truly works for you by paying attention to how things are unfolding—how things really feel, where your attention goes, and where your energy moves.

Most important, you gotta be willing to change, pivot, and readjust. Pivoting takes work and extra effort, and it might make you look like you don't know what you're doing—and who cares? No one fully knows what they're doing; everyone is figuring it out as they go. Trust that when things feel slow, there's a reason—and when you're ready for more, there will be more.

—Stefanie Raccuglia (she/her) LPC, LMHC, R-DMT

TEN PRINCIPLES OF PRIVATE PRACTICE

(1) IDENTIFY YOUR WHY + RETURN TO IT
What is at the core of why you are doing this work?

(2) BUILD AND PROTECT YOUR SELF-CARE PLAN
Make sure therapy is part of this plan at some point.

(3) CREATE AND LEAN ON YOUR SUPPORT SYSTEM
You do not have to do this alone. Who are your supports? Who/what else do you need?

(4) TALK TALK TALK ABOUT IT
How are you going to tell the world and your target audience what you are doing?

(5) GET INTIMATE WITH TALKING ABOUT MONEY
Finances can be difficult to talk about and you have to follow through. Pick your price and stick with it.

(6) SAYING NO IS ANOTHER WAY OF SAYING YES TO SOMETHING ELSE
Implement hours, a work number, refer out other resources, etc.

(7) YOUR ARE NOT FOR EVERYONE
And everyone is not for you, and that is okay and it will keep evolving.

(8) FIND SPACE, TAKE UP SPACE, MAKE SPACE, SHARE SPACE
Where will your business live? You deserve to take up space. How can you share space? Share business? Share resources?

(9) YOU ARE NOT JUST YOUR WORK
How can your work be a reflection of you and how can you not become over identified with your work?

(10) MOVE WITH INTENTION AND GET OUT OF YOUR OWN WAY
Move slow, trust yourself, if it is not a YES, pause. There will be time. Let things change.

EXERCISE 7

Name Your Business

Adapted from Day Corso's naming exercise, start with brainstorming what you hope the intention is for the name, use this exercise as a guide to identify your intention.

INTENTIONS

DESIRED IMPRESSION

The intention of how you want your brand to feel at the first impression.

____

____

____

DESIRED CULTURE AND PERSONA

The internal and external relationship of how your business operates/how that's seen.

____

____

____

DESIRED EMOTIONS OF EXPERIENCE

The intended emotions of what you want your potential and current clients to feel when interacting with your business.

____

____

____

BRAND EXPERIENCE

A focus on visual solution, voice, and tone.

____

____

____

Historically, folks we've worked with initially see this exercise as one of the fun ones. *I get to find a clever name for my business, awesome!* That is, until we shed light on all the intricacies of picking your business name, logo and more. When thinking about your private practice as a business, there are several ways you can go about picking a name.

But first, how to avoid the cliches. We invite you to jot down all the words that are overused, saturated, and cliche to therapy practices. These are probably words you want to avoid because of risks of brand confusion and trademarks by other established practices.

BRAND WORDS TO AVOID:

____

____

____

Words like *hope, thrive, catalyst, journey,* and *couch* are in use and very popular already. What can serve as an alternative for your practice to stand out amidst the noise?

Option 1: Go with your first name last name (counseling, therapeutic services, consulting). Example: Mary Smith Counseling, LLC. Intellectual Property Lawyers* tell us that no one can come after you for a business in your own name.

We are not lawyers, please consult one if you have questions. By "come after" we are talking about trademarks, where the entity that has successfully trademarked a name, logo, or slogan can send you a cease-and-desist letter or take you to court, forcing you to change your business name to something different.

Option 2: Have Artificial Intelligence (AI) suggest names. It's clunky and still has risks (read: trademarks) but it does result in some snickers and belly laughs.

Option 3: Write out all the words you are drawn to and start piecing them together. A second vital step is making sure no one has this name by doing 1) a quick internet search and 2) checking that there's no trademark preventing you from using this combo at https://www.uspto.gov/trademarks/search.

Option 4: Make up a word. Really! Just think of Google as the OG example. Nerd out over root words, play with unique spelling, and see what happens!

Before you make a final decision on your business name, use our name ranking guide (next page) for added clarity!

SPEAKING TO SUSTAINABILITY

When thinking about your name, think not just the here and now but how will your name change and evolve with you? Does it have room and flexibility?

- **Anyone starting their professional mental health career since 2020 is no one less than a brave spirit and light within this brutal world. Make sure to be gentle and caring to yourself. You and your work in the world are so needed.**

- **You are already enough, and never close off to learning throughout your career.**

- **Imposter syndrome is expected from time to time. While experiencing it may illuminate an area of growth to consider, know that it very well may be a reflection of just how much you care and invest in this sacred and significant work.**

—Evan Honerkamp, he/him, MA, LPC, ATR, EMDR-C, Studio Spectral PLLC

NAME RANKING

Add all possible names and rank.

Possible Name:

Does it explain your business purpose?	Is it universal and relatable?	Is it easier to remember?	Does it align with your intentions?
☐ Y ☐ N	☐ Y ☐ N	☐ Y ☐ N	☐ Y ☐ N

Possible Name:

Does it explain your business purpose?	Is it universal and relatable?	Is it easier to remember?	Does it align with your intentions?
☐ Y ☐ N	☐ Y ☐ N	☐ Y ☐ N	☐ Y ☐ N

Possible Name:

Does it explain your business purpose?	Is it universal and relatable?	Is it easier to remember?	Does it align with your intentions?
☐ Y ☐ N	☐ Y ☐ N	☐ Y ☐ N	☐ Y ☐ N

Possible Name:

Does it explain your business purpose?	Is it universal and relatable?	Is it easier to remember?	Does it align with your intentions?
☐ Y ☐ N	☐ Y ☐ N	☐ Y ☐ N	☐ Y ☐ N

If you had to pick today, which name would you pick?

____

EXERCISE 8

Color Psychology in Private Practice

Color Psychology can feel complimentary to accessibility needs when we think of the vulnerability, mental health, and safety needs found within our client population.
So let's start with a question:

What adjectives do you want clients to use to describe your office space? (If telehealth only, what message do you want to convey with the objects behind you in the video?)

____

____

____

____

____

____

____

Never have I (Khara) had a therapist answer this question with, "I want my client to find my office sterile." So what does it take to furnish or create a space aligned with your personality *and* therapeutic population? Let's start with colors.

What colors do you associate with therapy spaces? If you lease a space, they are usually beiges, taupes, and blues. Are these colors that align with your personality and the clientele you serve? No one said your office had to be boring!

Below are some common objects found in private practice offices:

☐ **COMFORTABLE FURNITURE OF EXPERIENCE**

Is it easily cleaned? Easy to get in and out of? Does it support all body types? Do you want two of the same chairs or is there clearly a therapist's chair? Is there a coffee table or other physical barriers? Why or why not?

☐ **SOFT LIGHTING**

Avoid harsh fluorescent lights that can cause headaches and aim for soft lighting. Do you want a daylight light bulb for winter months and Seasonal Affective Disorder (SAD)? Do you want a changing lightbulb or is that distracting?

☐ **TEXTURES**

If you want to avoid a harsh sterile environment, add textures in the pillows, blankets, and art you put in your space.

☐ **DESK OR WORKSPACE**

Is the desk for your administrative work? Would a client want to utilize the space for any of their work? What's on your desk and why? Hint: Clients notice a lot of things about your space, including any personal items on your desk.

☐ **SOUND MACHINE**

Is the sound machine effective at blocking out noise so your client can do hard work with big emotions without worrying about being heard?

☐ **BOOKS**

Clients pay attention to the books on your shelves. What messages are you conveying through the books you include? Inclusivity? Confidence in a topic?

☐ **ARTWORK**

Is the art you include special to you? Are you comfortable with clients asking about it? Is it cliche nature pictures or something else that clients would find distracting vs. helpful? Are you supporting a local artist?

☐ **PLANTS**

Great for oxygen and keeping a space friendly and approachable, are your plants alive or fake based on windows and light in your office? Are there allergies you need to consider?

☐ **ESSENTIAL OILS**

Are there allergies you need to remain aware of? How would your office mates respond to smells? Anticipating client sensitivity to smells?

☐ **FIDGET OBJECTS AND SENSORY TOOLS**

What objects and sensory tools could be helpful to have in your space? Weighted blankets? Fidgets? Lotion? Mints? Water or tea?

☐   ____

☐   ____

☐   ____

If you do a specialized type of therapy, of course you may have even more things in your office than what are included here. Items like a light bar, buzzers, play therapy toys, sand tray figurines, and more. Add to the list above to represent the type of work you do and the population you serve.

SPEAKING TO SUSTAINABILITY

What in your space supports inclusivity and accessibility to the client population(s) you serve? Are you willing to make changes to be more inclusive in your space? What products are you using that are sustainable? As you are buying things for your space, are you supporting local, or can you?

Starting a private practice is an exciting opportunity to create a space that truly reflects who you are as a therapist and the values that guide your work. Take time to explore the type of therapy that feels most meaningful to you and the clients you feel most connected with. Developing a clear specialty allows you to build a caseload that aligns with your strengths and passions, making your work more fulfilling and sustainable. It also helps you attract clients who are looking for the kind of therapy you genuinely want to provide. When your practice is intentionally shaped around the work you care about most, it becomes a space where both you and your clients can do your best work.

—Cass Daniels (he/him) LCSW

EXERCISE 9

Knowing Your Numbers: Budgeting in Private Practice

There are three types of expenses to consider in private practice, including start-up costs, monthly expenses, and periodic expenses. Let's look at each of them to help you prepare financially for this business investment, without financial stress or going into unexpected debt.

Example Private Practice Start-Up Costs

☐   State-specific mental health paperwork (disclosure, consent, PHI, HIPAA, telehealth)

☐   Telehealth gear (light ring, laptop stand, earbuds/headphones)

☐   Office furnishings if offering in-person services (chairs, desk, lamps, art, plants)

☐   Electronic Health Record (SimplePractice, Owl, Jane, TherapyNotes, TherapyPartner)

☐   Malpractice insurance (in your name and your business name)

☐   Registration for your business in your state

☐   EIN (free!)

☐   Organizational NPI (free!)

☐   Cost of credentialing with insurances (if applicable)

☐   Cost of website design

☐   Website domain purchased

☐   Confidential email/messaging/voicemail

☐   Marketing materials

☐   Professional Association Fees (APA, ACA, NASW)

☐   Cushion of 2-3 months income to keep business going

☐   ____

What needs to be added to this list for you? Client supplies? Play therapy supplies? EMDR buzzers? Art materials? Add to the list!

Next, research and reflect the cost of these things, writing the estimated amount next to each item. How much do you need to save to get this ball rolling? Do you want to (or need to) take out a small business loan? Or is it about creating a plan to save ahead of time for the launch?

Speaking of saving ahead of time, you'll also want to factor in a cushion of several months to pay yourself AND cover the expenses of the business as you build your caseload. You are a business owner now, we don't want to create poor habits like not paying yourself because the launch process makes money feel tight. This intention supports preparation over reaction.

And now let's look at repeated expenses to maintain your business:

Example Monthly Expenses

☐ Office rent	☐ Payroll (paying yourself!!)
☐ Electronic Health Record (EHR)	☐ Business savings (think Paid Time Off (PTO) and emergencies)
☐ Credit card processing fees	
☐ Office utilities	☐ Private supervision
☐ Coffee/tea (if in-person)	☐ _________________________
☐ Marketing	☐ _________________________
☐ Online directory listings	☐ _________________________
☐ Phone/fax	☐ _________________________
☐ Continued education	☐ _________________________
☐ Taxes	☐ _________________________

How are you feeling with these monthly expenses? Add them up to estimate how much you need to bring in to keep the business going AND pay yourself!

Finally, the periodic expenses are what trip up even the best budgeters we know. Here are some examples of periodic expenses in private practice to remain aware of:

Example Periodic Expenses

☐   Legal consultation/fees

☐   Continued education/trainings/ retreats

☐   Malpractice insurance

☐   Annual renewals for software

☐   Tax Filing/Accountant Fees

☐   Conferences

☐   Bigger marketing efforts

☐   Videography

☐   Business coach/practice coach

☐   Consultation

☐   ___________________________

☐   ___________________________

☐   ___________________________

☐   ___________________________

Do you have a clearer sense of your startup costs, monthly expenses, and periodic expenses? Write the estimated amounts below for additional processing of any thoughts and feelings that come up. What are you thinking when seeing each number? What are you feeling and where do you feel that in your body? What plans do you need in place to feel good about the costs of your business?

Startup costs: $ ____

Monthly expenses: $ ____

Periodic expenses: $ ____

Don't forget to pay yourself!

You'll notice we factored in payroll (paying yourself) as a monthly expense. It's usually the first thing therapists forgo when money is feeling stretched too thin. How much do you want to pay yourself? Is there a salary you are aiming for? There are multiple ways to go about this number. One is to take the salary you want to bring home and go backwards until you calculate your hourly client rate. As a financial therapist, I (Khara) encourage people to start with two more quality-of-life questions:

1. How many clients do you want to see a week?
2. How many weeks (out of 52 weeks) do you want to work per year?

From there, we can do some math or use an awesome income calculator to identify how much you need to charge per client hour for ongoing exploration!

Want a more heart-felt exploration for setting (or raising) your rates? Check out the next exercise!

SPEAKING TO SUSTAINABILITY

Paying yourself is often the first thing therapists stop doing when money feels scarce. What plans can you put in place to ensure you are paying yourself fairly and regularly? Money is one kind of wealth and in capitalism it is a very important one. The more income you have, the more you are able to pay people for their work, model for your clients that they also deserve to be paid, and support your community. Money is not a bad thing; it can be empowering and allows you to do your work, share your wealth, and support others to do the same.

Psychotherapy is a profession unlike any other. We sit with people one-on-one with our full, undivided attention, our advanced clinical training, and our commitment to unconditional positive regard. This is sacred work. It deserves to be sustained, and we deserve to be well-resourced in order to continue offering it. One of the most powerful ways we do this is by charging fees that allow us to thrive. When we are well-resourced, we can stay in right relationship with ourselves, our clients, and the work.

—Abby Howard, MSW, LCSW (she/her/hers) Abby Howard Counseling

EXERCISE 10

Self-Worth and Setting Rates

Consider the following quadrants and what you would put in each box. What thoughts and feelings are coming up as you move from box 1 to box 4?

Therapist Self-Worth Exercise

Quadrant 1: "Self of Therapist"
Explore: Who am I?
Lived Experience
Therapeutic Style
Personality

Quadrant 2: "My Training"
Identify Level of Experience
Licensure
Trainings & Certifications
Years in the Field

Quadrant 3: "My Specialties"
Define Niches
Preferred Populations
Client Pain Points
Supervision/Consultation

Quadrant 4: "My Location"
Conduct Market Research
Average Cost Per Session
Insurance Reimbursement Comparison
"Competitors" and Colleagues

What clarity did you gain from this exercise when setting or raising your rates? If you are planning to raise your rates, what strategies have you considered?

Strategy #1: Raise everyone on your caseload, as well as new clients by $5-15 on a set date.

Strategy #2: Raise rates for new clients only.

Financial psychology tells us that folks are most comfortable with an increase between $5 and $10 at a time. Psychology also tells us that people want the rate increase spelled out. Consider a notice that says we are raising your rate by 5% vs. $5. Five dollars is easy to understand whereas 5% takes some math which can result in anxiety and overreaction as people stop to calculate what they need to pay. Make it more painless by naming the rate increase, the new rate, and the date the new rate goes into effect. For example:

Hello!

I value our work together and wanted to provide ample notice of my rates increasing effective September 1st. Your rate of $XXX for (service) is increasing (by $5-15) to $XXX. Please let me know what questions you have, I am open to exploring your thoughts and concerns in our next session on (date).

Warmly,
Your Name

Notice the language choice is careful to not have clients assuming they can negotiate the rate increase. This invitation is not an opportunity for them to barter or talk down the price of therapy after you went through the detailed process of establishing your new rate. Instead, the processing offered in the example above is for any emotional responses (anxiety, fear, stress) they want to name as part of the therapeutic relationship. Or to declare they need to move to biweekly or monthly to maintain therapy with you. Sometimes it could be a discussion of needing to transfer to another therapist with a lower rate.

With that being said, here are some things to remember about clients and therapy:

1. They don't like to start over if they like their therapist and can afford to stay

2. They can move to biweekly or monthly if that would support their budget

3. Some folks use HSA funds to pay for therapy

4. Some folks might see this as an opportunity to wrap up therapy

Oddly enough, the colleagues I (Khara) have worked with to thoughtfully raise their rates anticipated some sort of conflict with clients, such as the client accusing them of being greedy, overpriced, or selfish (thanks inner critic and noble poverty) only to have clients say "okay, I understand," with minimal disruption and back to business as usual.

Outside of matter-of-fact business coaches who chirp "just raise your rates" to therapists left and right, no one is saying raising your rates is easy. It causes lots of anxiety for most therapists. And that doesn't mean we shouldn't raise our rates in cash pay practices just to avoid anticipated conflict that might not actually happen.

Some colleagues we know raise their rates yearly, whereas others raise them more or less frequently based on life factors, comfort, and the clientele they serve. By looking at your quadrants as well as the expenses and/or income calculator in the last exercise, are you charging what you need to make ends meet? If raising your rates isn't an option, how else can you generate additional income to support yourself and your business? Check out our secondary income exercise further in this workbook!

SPEAKING TO SUSTAINABILITY

The mental health field is consistently underpaid and overworked, resulting in high burn out and people leaving the field or doing subpar or even poor clinical work. Setting our rates reflects the value placed on therapy, even when we are an insurance-based practice. Charging what you're worth can be reflected to insurance panels in your claims, even when their contracted rates to pay you are insultingly low. Providing more data to insurance panels on what therapists are charging for therapy can help them offer rate increases to the mental health professionals paneled to do this important work.

Be bold with your courage to break the constructs- "time on/ time off", "success", "what you think you're worth or deserve", "what you should or should not share on your website". And be bold enough to claim that you are a business owner—having a private practice does in fact make you an entrepreneur, so act like one—embody it—and also keep learning. Take courses, read, consult with others, get familiar with the parts of having a business that you might not like so much. As Liz Gilbert says, and I'm paraphrasing here—there are always shit sandwiches ya gotta eat that come with doing the things you love and want.

There will be days when you're either working on your business, in your business or for your business—and in any of those scenarios—your working. Keep that in mind when you feel the productivity-shame gremlin in your mind. And most important remember that you need **TRUE** breaks where you're just letting your business do its thing. Having your own practice is a 24/7 relationship but you don't need to be efforting 24/7, let the relationship be mutual and reciprocal.

—Stefanie Raccuglia (she/her) LPC, LMHC, R-DMT

EXERCISE 11

PsychologyToday Bingo and Your Website Copy

Check out the BINGO board below. What stands out to you? Why would we include these words on our problematic bingo card? Just like we saw with naming your business in an earlier exercise, there are overused or unclear words that add to the noise or contribute confusion when attempting to connect with potential clients. Oftentimes your online profile is where clients find you first, so why not speak directly to them?

PROBLEMATIC PROFILE BINGO

Focus on credentials	Life transitions	Healing
CBT, DBT, EMDR	Path	Tons of acronyms
Better you	Thrive	Have hope

Take a look at our 'report card' below. What about other therapist profiles online? Consider how your online profile measures up.

ONLINE PROFILE REPORT CARD

Profile Elements to Include	Question	Not at all (1)	Maybe (2)	Somewhat (3)	Absolutely (4)
Greeting to Ideal Client	Does their profile start with an engaging statement that speaks to their ideal client?				
Client-focused Language	Does their profile speak to an ideal client in language that client would relate to?				
Location and Telehealth Indicated	Is it clear if they offer in person, telehealth, or both?				
Pricing and Insurances Accepted	Does their profile indicate the cost of sessions and any insurance they may accept?				
Profile Picture	Is there a profile picture that reflects a clinicians' personality and professionalism?				
Bonus: Video Clip and/or office pictures	Do they go above and beyond to help a potential client get to know them through video or showing off their office style?				

OVERALL SCORE	NOTES:

What adjustments can be made to help your profile stand out as a true representation of the meaningful work you do? Additionally, how can the adjustments to your online profile help you write some solid website copy? Consider the formula for a memorable PsychologyToday profile below:

Paragraph 1:
- Hook (question/stat)
- Who you work with
- What you help them achieve

Paragraph 2:
- Your expertise and credentials, your therapeutic approach, a Call-To-Action such as 'book a free consult, visit my website.'

How would this look as website copy or as a social media post? Here are a couple examples:

Do you struggle to turn off your brain after long work days? Do you think about work constantly, even when you are off the clock? I work with high-achieving entrepreneurs who struggle with perfectionism, workaholism, and anxiety to discover work-life harmony so they don't burn out of their career before turning fifty.

My name is _______________ and as a former workaholic, perfectionist entrepreneur myself, I've identified strategies that work for busy professionals to experience purpose and fulfillment in their work and homelife. I am trained in the Enneagram, EMDR, and IFS parts work with a therapeutic approach of building a strong therapeutic relationship for you to do the deeper work you haven't had the space and time to do alone. Let's chat!

Are you grieving the loss of someone who is still alive? Did you have a strained family dynamic? I work with adults who've experienced complex trauma and estrangement to help you reparent yourself and heal your childhood wounds.

Hi my name is _______________ and I value working with LGBTQ+, neurodivergent, and creative adults ages 18-55. My therapeutic approaches include psychoanalytic, IFS, and Brainspotting. Reach out to see if I'm the right fit for your goals by emailing me at _______________ .

Now it's your turn! Write your first draft on the lines on this page:

Remember Paragraph 1:	*Paragraph 2:*
Hook (question/stat)	*Your expertise and credentials, your therapeutic*
Who you work with	*approach, a Call-To-Action such as 'book a free*
What you help them achieve	*consult, visit my website.'*

____

____

____

____

____

____

SPEAKING TO SUSTAINABILITY

How can your website or online directory copy be friendly, approachable, and clearly speak to the audience you want to serve as a therapist? Is there language to embrace? Words to avoid? Images to include? Read what you wrote out loud to explore the tone of voice and to make sure it sounds like you.

This is going to be hard and it might not be immediate, but you will find what works for you. Marketing is your new best friend, but luckily you have control and can decide how you want to make it all happen. You do not need to pay a ton of money for a coach, you can if you want to, but above all you have to feel aligned with what you are trying to create and sometimes that involves trial and error.

—Aja Evans, she/her, LMHC, Financial Therapist

EXERCISE 12

Identifying Your Ideal Client

Why is it important to niche down and identify your ideal client or clients? Not only does it help you speak to the people you want to work with most in marketing like your website copy and social media presence/posts, it also helps colleagues remember you as a potential fit for clients they come across in business.

HINT: A lot of therapists can work with trauma, anxiety, depression, and life transitions. Getting more specific helps people find you!

Use the template below to help you identify why your ideal client is coming to therapy, any barriers to the work, and the language of what they are seeking from therapy services to help you speak clearly to them about what you do. This then helps you solidify messaging and marketing to have the folks you love to work with most fill up your caseload!

Here's a simple starting question: of the types of clients you've worked with in the past, which ones did you feel most energized or fulfilled by? Which clients did you feel you did your best work with and why?

Who do you want to work with now? You are allowed to have multiple ideal clients AND you are also allowed to pivot as seasons change or your needs evolve.

SPEAKING TO SUSTAINABILITY

Are there other features, interests, or needs for your ideal client that you'd add to this exercise? Do you have lived experience similar to your ideal client and if so, is that important to convey in marketing?

Remember to be human. It's the greatest superpower you have as a therapist!

—Jenny Hughes, PhD, Founder of The BRAVE Trauma Therapist Collective

IDEAL CLIENT PROFILE

GOALS AND VALUES

Goals:

Values:

Age:

Sexual
Orientation:

Gender:

Race/Ethnicity:

Location:

Relationship
Status:

#/Age of
Children:

Language:

Socio Economic
Status:

Occupation:

Level of
Education:

Anything Else:

CHALLENGES &
PAIN POINTS

Challenges:

Pain Points:

SOURCES OF
INFORMATION

Books:

Magazines:

Blogs/Websites:

Conferences:

Experts/Influencers:

Other:

OBJECTIONS & ROLE IN
PURCHASE PROCESS

Objections to the sale/service:

Role in the purchase process:

EXERCISE 13

Elevator Pitch Practice

A pitch is a short statement that conveys what we do, for whom, and how. It's meant to be said with enthusiasm. It's also meant to be 23 words or less so the listener can remember it. Here's the formula:

I help ___________ (who) achieve ___________ (what) by ___________ (strategies/tools/modality)

A great tool for introductions and networking events, here are some examples of pitches:

- I help burned out therapists create secondary income streams for work-life harmony and financial stability so they don't have to work so hard.

- I help millennial moms redefine themselves postpartum through person-centered approaches and ceremony to witness their transformation.

- I help college-aged students adjust to their new beginnings through life quakes grief work and Enneagram-informed therapy.

- I help men struggling with anger to communicate effectively with their partners for meaningful relationships by shedding toxic masculinity.

Ready to give it a try? Fill in the blanks until you get a pitch you feel heartfelt about!

I help ___________ (who) achieve ___________ (what) by ___________ (strategies/tools/modality)

I help ___________ achieve ___________ by ___________

I help ___________ achieve ___________ by ___________

I help ___________ achieve ___________ by ___________

I help ___________ achieve ___________ by ___________

I help ___________ achieve ___________ by ___________

44

 ## SPEAKING TO SUSTAINABILITY

Is your pitch memorable? Authentic? Enthusiastically delivered? Keep working on it until you feel energized by it.

More clients are not necessarily better than fewer clients who are a good fit. Networking is key. Join a consult group or list serve. Try to find your niche and a professional community. Use technology to support the parts of being in private practice that are hard or not your strengths. Go to conferences. Apply to present at conferences. Look for public speaking or educational opportunities that can help legitimize you and get your name out.

—Anonymous

EXERCISE 14

Selecting Supports

Although private practice can feel lonely, you don't have to navigate it alone. Below is an exercise in finding supports. What questions do you need to ask? After all, you are interviewing them for fit as much as they are learning about you!

My Supports in Private Practice

Legal Team	**Accounting Professional(s)**
Who do they work with?	Who do they work with?
Resources to clients?	What services do they offer?
Location?	Types of businesses they serve
Paperwork provided?	Fee structure
Court participation?	

Consultant(s)	**Colleagues**
Skills they bring to consultation	Emotional support
Services they offer	Professional Will Executor
Availability	Time off coverage
Fee structure	Perspective and Mutually beneficial

Have some folks in mind? If you are feeling stuck, check out directories for therapists or ask colleagues who they love working with. The biggest aspect to emphasize is that you want professionals well-versed in working with therapists in private practice. Your aunt's brother's cousin the accountant is not going to cut it if they have no experience in working with private practice therapists, trust us on this one.

Where else can you see these professionals in action? Private practice podcasts! Check out podcasts like the ones below for free information or just a vibe check before outreaching one of the professionals featured for more information on how to work with them:

The Private Practice Pro

Heard Business School

Money Nuts and Bolts for Therapists

All Things Private Practice

The Group Practice Exchange

The Productive Therapist

Our colleague highlighted 11 podcasts on private practice at https://productivetherapist. com/the-11-best-business-podcasts-for-therapists/

SPEAKING TO SUSTAINABILITY

How important is representation in the supports you engage? Do you have questions for them on their clientele, diversity, and accessibility? Write out your interview questions so you can feel as prepared as possible before meeting with them.

I have three pieces to share: 1) Build a community of trusted colleagues, including supervisors/consultants and referral sources. 2) Be curious about your own practice and ask for feedback about your work. 3) Keep learning! Continue to ask questions, seek professional development opportunities, stay up to date on trends in the field, and know that there's always something you can learn from others.

—Ashley Charbonneau, LCSW

EXERCISE 15

Burnout Prevention (Not If, But When)

Burnout will happen in this work. It's a matter of not 'if' but 'when.' So we want to give you tools and strategies to get ahead of it, while reminding you that if you feel burnt out, you are probably days, weeks, or months beyond needing a break.

This field and world are dictated by an urgent pace that was designed to make us feel like we cannot stop, but here is the truth: if you don't figure out how to rest or take time off, you will end up in a place of not wanting or being able to continue this work. And yet you felt called to do this work, so learning how to slow down, rest, and take time away from it is essential.

Part I: Burnout Prevention Tools

- Out of office message

- Scaling level of enjoyment

- Identify your signs of burnout

Crafting Your Out of Office Message

Utilizing your out of office function on your email is one way we all can prevent burnout by modeling what it looks like to step away from the business for an hour, a day, a weekend, or for some planned time off. Below is a formula of what to include when deploying this as a healthy boundary with others in your business.

- Statement of dates you are out

- Indication of when you will return/answer emails

- Emergency contact information, coverage therapist if applicable, other mental health resources

Here are two colleague examples:

Hello!
Thank you for reaching out. I will be out of the office and not responding to emails beginning
Thursday, April 21- May 3rd.

If you would like to request an appointment online, you may do so here: _______________

If you are an existing client and experiencing a crisis, please call 988 or head directly to your
nearest crisis center or emergency room. Colorado Crisis Services Number: 1-844-493-8255

Thank you for connecting with me at ABC Counseling! I am currently out of the office and have
received your email with plans to respond within the 48 business hours of my return.
If this is an emergency, please use an appropriate resource below:

988
911
Colorado Crisis Services: 1.844.493.8255 or Text "TALK" to 38255
Safe2Tell Colorado:1.877.542.7233
National Suicide Prevention Lifeline: 1.800.273.8255
The Trevor Project (LGBTQIA+ Focus):1.866.488.7386

Out of office messages can also be utilized when naming that you are away for things like family
time or child pickup, a conference or training, or just to let the sender know your policy for returning
emails, such as responding within 72 hours or on business days (indicating you don't respond on
weekends or planned days off). Below is an example of a message that one colleague sends to
confirm an email is received while also indicating healthy boundaries around response times:

*Message received! I'm excited to connect with you further and typically I respond to most emails within
48 hours. I value your time and respect your boundaries. If you happen to receive this message while
taking time off from work, please feel free to respond as soon as you can. Reply when you can, and I will
do the same.*

Now it's your turn! What would a drafted message look like for planned time off? Craft it below?

And what about a message indicating your availability to respond to new inquiries or emails that you receive at any hour of the day? Craft it below.

Scaling Your Level of Enjoyment

Just because a private practice therapist is a business owner doesn't mean we enjoy all aspects of business. Another tool in support of burnout prevention is scaling your level of enjoyment for each activity, with plans to delegate on a timeline that feels financially and logically appropriate.

Consider all the things you do when working ON your business rather than in it. Write them down. Next, put a number next to each one, with 1 being you don't enjoy that task at all, and 10 being that you enjoy it immensely.

What do you notice?

Take note of anything that is ranked as 5 or below on the enjoyableness scale. These items might be worth delegating at some point in your business future to a support person or service in order to reduce burnout potential.

Identify Your Signs of Burnout

Consider the importance of identifying your own signs of burnout by reflecting on the questions below. After all, if you don't recognize your signs of burnout, how can you work on them? What stands out to you in your responses? Who can you share this exercise with in order to support your own burnout prevention and/or recovery as a clinician in the mental health field?

What does burnout look like for me?

Physical Signs of Burnout (i.e. fatigue, muscle aches, headaches, weight changes)

____

Emotional Signs of Burnout (i.e irritability, easier to cry, numbness, increased road rage)

____

Mental Signs of Burnout (i.e. brain fog, loss of focus, difficulty remembering things)

____

Existential/Spiritual Signs of Burnout (i.e. feeling jaded about the work, critical, questioning purpose)

____

Burnout Signs at Work (i.e. not completing notes, relief when a client cancels, dread)

____

Burnout Signs in my Relationships (i.e. withdrawing, having nothing to give, annoyed)

____

Part II: R&R Redefined

You've heard about R&R as rest and relaxation. Yet for many therapists, it's hard to relax when building your business, or even after attending to your clients needs. What if you struggle with self-care like so many clinicians do? Enter restoration.

The question to ask yourself: What energizes me? What builds me back up? What restores me? The good news is that folks' answers to this question are usually accessible and affordable, more so than the commercialized activities people first think of as self-care.

Now organize some activities into each box below, with things you do 'solo' as alone activities, and 'together' represents with other people. Additionally, 'quiet' indicates low energy and 'active' signifies higher energy.

	QUIET	ACTIVE
ALONE	*Examples: Reading, Journaling, Creating*	*Examples: Walking or jogging, Solo dance party, Cleaning*
TOGETHER	*Examples: Watching a movie, Listening to music, Going for a drive*	*Examples: Fitness class, Cooking, Legos and games*

Do any of your boxes need some attention? Do you have plenty of ideas for one area of self-care but not another? Now that you have ideas written down, keep them someplace handy for reference.

Lastly, if you don't schedule it, it doesn't happen. So where can you put some R&R in your schedule in the next week?

 ## SPEAKING TO SUSTAINABILITY

There are many books on burnout, so what we will say here is that burnout is a symptom of capitalism and urgency culture. Burnout is the impact of trying to keep up in a world that wants us to feel deficient in our productivity and worth! Finding ways you can take care of yourself so you do not burnout is vital so that you continue doing what feels meaningful personally and professionally.

Ask yourself, 'Is this productivity or busyness?' One leads to increased fulfillment, the other leads to burnout.

—Khara Croswaite Brindle, MA, LPC, ACS, CFT, TEDx Speaker on *The Burden of Busyness*

EXERCISE 16

Contingency Planning

It's hard to hold the excitement of building a business with the stress of something challenging its ability to succeed. Especially since many of us don't enjoy sitting in the discomfort of imagining all the horrible things that could happen. Let's normalize that things do happen, including joyful or awful career-altering things that could result in our businesses pausing for a time, pivoting, or closing. Things like:

- Battling cancer
- Chronic illness
- A sudden death
- Caregiving
- Trauma

- Childbirth
- Postpartum depression
- Mental health crisis
- Clinician death
- A pandemic

One of our goals with this workbook is to help clinicians launching their private practice feel as prepared as possible, which should include the events that we don't often want to think about. What if we had a plan for when things get uncomfortable? What if we had instructions for what to do if we became incapacitated? Enter the professional will.

A professional will identifies a clinical colleague who will take the reins of managing your business should you become incapacitated or die. It may also be worthwhile to have a colleague in mind for when things get stressful and you need to scale back or step away from your business for a brief pause. Although we aren't lawyers, it's been recommended to pick a professional who:

- Understands our business (and often isn't a family member)
- Agrees to outreach clients should they need to be notified of a change
- Help clients connect with new providers should we be unable to continue our services with them

To help them help you, a professional will should outline where important information is located, as well as steps you'd like the professional to take regarding your business. Take a look at the following template courtesy of Fida Law to consider your responses, and fill in the blanks. What else needs to be included to support your business?

PROFESSIONAL WILL

I, ____, do hereby declare this to be my
Professional Will. This document supersedes any prior Professional Will(s). This document is not
my last Will and Testament. This Professional Will is intended to give authority and directions to
my Executor named in this Professional Will to matters in connection with my practice and client
records in the event of my incapacitation or death.

FIRST

I am a practicing _____________________ licensed in _____________________. My license # is
_____________________. My principal office address is _____________________. In the event of my
death or incapacitation, I hereby appoint as my Professional Executor _____________________, who
has agreed to serve in this role. His/her telephone number, email address, and mailing address are

____.

In the event that _____________________ is unavailable or unable to perform this function, I
hereby appoint as Secondary Professional Executor _____________________, who has
agreed to serve in this role. His/her telephone number, email address, and mailing address are

____.

I hereby grant my Professional Executors full authority to:

_____ Act on my behalf in making decisions about storing, releasing, and/or disposing of my
professional records and client records, consistent with the applicable federal and state laws
and regulations, and other professional requirements.
_____ Carry out any activities deemed necessary to administer this Professional Will.
_____ Delegate and authorize other people so designated and determined by them to assist and
perform any requisite activities to properly administer this Professional Will.

SECOND

My attorney for this Professional Will is _____________________ .
His/her telephone number, email address, and mailing address are

____.

The Executor of my current personal Will is_____________________.
His/her telephone number, email address, and mailing address are

____.

THIRD

Copies of a separate list of files, passwords, contact list, and client list are stored with copies of
my Professional Will in the locations stated in section FOURTH (A). This list includes: names and
contact information of individuals who may assist in locating and accessing my client records and

other relevant professional documents; locations and how to access all client records; locations and how to access my professional billing and financial records, appointment book, client telephone numbers and related contact information; the location of the computer and other electronic devices used for my practice; passwords for my computer and other electronic devices used for my practice; my professional email and website address with passwords and codes; my office telephone numbers and voicemail access codes; location of my insurance policies and related documentation; location of any necessary keys and combinations required for access to my office, filing storage units, and facilities.

FOURTH

A. There are four copies of this Professional Will located as follows: with my attorney,

____.

B. Use your professional judgment and discretion regarding notification existing and past clients of my death or incapacity and who to contact consistent with ethical and legal requirements.

C. Subject to clinical indications, my Professional Executor or those professionals appointed and referred there from, may offer personal counseling to certain clients as duly specified by my Professional Executor.

D. Notify my insurance carrier(s) of my death and arrange for coverage as appropriate and prorated refunds to my Estate as appropriate. Also notify the State Licensing Board.

E. Arrange for each client's records to go to their new practitioner if applicable, with each client's consent. All remaining records must be maintained pursuant to state and federal laws and regulations.

F. My Estate is to be billed for all expenses incurred and services rendered on its behalf by my Attorney at the rate of _____________________, and by my Professional Executor at the rate of _____________________. All other expenses and services performed on behalf of my Estate are to be billed to my Estate at a reasonable cost.

I declare that the foregoing is true and correct.

Executed at ____, on _____________________.

Signature: ____

WITNESSES

Printed Name: _____________________________ Signature: _________________ Date: ___________

Address: ____

Printed Name: _____________________________ Signature: _________________ Date: ___________

Address: ____

SPEAKING TO SUSTAINABILITY

How will your work or your business continue forward without you? Who can help when something happens where you need to step away or take a break? Consider how you would ask for help, and from whom.

A professional will or contingency plan is not just tedious paperwork. It is an important way of future-proofing your practice, and more importantly, it is one of the last, quiet acts of care we can offer our clients. Planning for incapacity or death may feel uncomfortable, but it is also one of the most compassionate and ethical steps we can take to ensure clients are not left without support when they need stability the most.

—Cathy Wilson, LPC, ACS, PFVC Author, Educator, and Counselor in Littleton, Colorado

EXERCISE 17

Building Secondary Income Streams

Let's start with a visualization exercise. Sit back, get in a comfy position, and close your eyes or put them at rest. If money wasn't a stressor (as in your financial needs are met) what would you like to do for four hours a day?

Journal your response:

____

____

____

____

____

____

____

____

____

Did anything about your response surprise you? Did it provide insight into what you'd like to add or take away in your private practice as a business? Are you burning out? Is there something you want to move toward as a future goal?

The modern therapist doesn't aspire to see 25-35 clients a week indefinitely. Although 20-25 is considered "full" in private practice, the amount of clients you can sustain is based on your availability, stamina, health, and so many other factors. And for most of us, we can't raise our rates to $400 an hour and expect to have a full caseload.

Therefore it's important to normalize additional income streams as part of your business model. Partly as burnout prevention, and partly for feeding your creativity and bringing the balance of joy to the hard work of being a therapist!

There are two types of income streams: active and passive. Burned out therapists want passive income because it wouldn't take more energy from them. Yet most income streams start active, as in they take time to build, launch, and market, and then eventually have the ability to become passive. Passive income, by definition, means you launch the offering and it does its own thing to bring you income. In our experience, passive income streams take 3-4 years to truly be passive. But don't let that dissuade you, that's why we want to start thinking of your income streams now!

Receiving notifications of someone buying something you created can bring a dose of dopamine as you go about your life. So what are some examples of passive versus active income streams? There's a world of possibilities (and blogs of ideas) out there, so we will just name a few:

Passive

- Book or workbook sales
- On-demand courses
- Digital downloads
- Royalties from co-created courses
- Sponsorships on your podcast or Youtube channel

Active

- Teaching/adjunct faculty
- Speaking
- Workshops
- Live training
- Retreats
- Podcasts

- YouTube
- Swag
- Influencer

- Consultant
- Coach
- Supervisor

Of course there are other income streams completely unrelated to your mental health background. Things like real estate, investments, ride shares, etsy shops, second jobs, and more. Did any of the examples from the lists above align with your interests from the 4-hours-a-day exercise? Although we want to keep some of your passions and hobbies sacred, some of your interests could translate to additional income!

Here are some others questions to explore your secondary income potential:

1. What exercises, tools, metaphors, or analogies do I introduce to clients again and again. Do I put my own spin on them?

2. What do colleagues or community members ask me based on my expertise?

3. What's the gift I'm giving clients when they work with me? Is that scalable?

Although these questions may feel quirky, they are getting to the root of your special gifts and interests, as well as looking at pain points within your community. A pain point is an unmet need in business speak. And you have the solution! Are you talking about or serving a population that is underserved? Does your metaphor or a way of working with people that deserves to be introduced to other therapists as another valuable tool in their toolkit? Now you are starting to see how the pain points transform into possibilities!

So now that you are getting some ideas, where in your schedule is there a 2-hour block to work ON your business rather than in it? As consultants to therapists, we've seen colleagues enthusiasm to build new things, but if there isn't time in their schedule, there's no movement.

Look at your calendar and find a two hour block to work on building your income stream, whether that's writing, creating, researching, recording, or marketing. If you don't schedule it, it doesn't happen.

SPEAKING TO SUSTAINABILITY

What populations need your gifts packaged in accessible and affordable ways? Is there a way to scale the difference you are making by teaching other mental health professionals a tool or technique?

It's imperative to have outlets that not only provide secondary income, but also feed your soul and replenishes your heart, mind, and body—especially if they are aligned with your values!

—Alejandro Castro, LPC, LAC, Owner of Transcending Consultation Group

EXERCISE 18

Sustainable Urgency and Work-Life Harmony

The term sustainable urgency is both a reminder and a practice: to slow down and work against urgency culture and the attention economy. It invites you to adjust your pace so you can act in ways that are congruent with your needs and feelings, supporting yourself, your long-term self, and the community around you. When we live in a culture ,and work in a field, where everything feels urgent, it can be difficult to find your own rhythm and trust yourself.

Below are questions to help you apply Sustainable Urgency to your work. (For more on this framework, see Sam's other writing at Samfieldtherapy.com.)

- WHAT IS SUSTAINABLE TO YOU?

- WHAT IS NOT SUSTAINABLE FOR YOU?

- WHAT IS URGENT TO YOU?

- WHAT IS NOT URGENT FOR YOU?

- When something is urgent for someone else, but not you, how do you respond? Is this how you want to continue to respond at this moment?

- WHAT IMPACTS YOUR SENSE OF URGENCY AND/OR SUSTAINABILITY?

- What feelings need space when you feel urgent in order for your to respond in a way that honors yourself, your future self, and your community?

MY PERSONAL WELLNESS PLAN
Supporting Self-Care

Wellness Recovery

Another piece to the private practice puzzle is knowing when things are off-kilter. Such as when you are burning the candle at both ends. Or when things are feeling unmanageable and overwhelming. Enter the Wellness Recovery Action Plan (WRAP)! This is a self-care strategy that invites a person to think about their warning signs for burnout ahead of time, and then map out their plan for coming back to center. Your invitation is to reflect on the content for each box and write it out, then share it with a loved one who you trust can help you get back on track if you need support to do so.

What does it look like when I'm well? Physical? Emotional? Intellectual? Spiritual?	**What does it look like when I'm not well?** Physical? Emotional? Intellectual? Spiritual?
Warning signs (internal)	**Triggers (external)**
My supports Primary: Secondary: Relationships I want to strengthen:	**When things are breaking down**
Plan of Action: How do I get back to well?	**What do I need from others?**

 ## SPEAKING TO SUSTAINABILITY

Speaking to Sustainability: The WRAP is applicable for folks of all different backgrounds. Khara was first introduced to it by case managers with the Department of Human Services, who were then introducing it to community members experiencing housing insecurity. How can this plan be useful to you AND your clients?

We live in a time that demands urgency, but our nervous systems were not built for it. Slowing down is not avoidance—it's how we care for ourselves, our futures, and our communities.

—Sam Field, MA, LPC, LAC, Field Therapy

EXERCISE 19

Interviewing Your Community

Private practice can be lonely without professional supports and colleagues to connect with on our journey. Fortunately, there are many clinicians who feel passionately about giving back to their community by sharing their wisdom and stories of lessons learned in business. Below is a list of questions that might help you connect further with your community. Engaging your community could lead to burnout prevention, referrals, and future business opportunities.

What initially drew you to the field of therapy, and how has that motivation evolved over time?

What were the most influential experiences, personal or professional, that shaped your decision to become a therapist?

What surprised you most about graduate training or the early stages of your career?

How did you choose your specific modalities or areas of specialization, and what guided those decisions? How has it shifted?

What challenges did you face during your training or licensure process, and how did you navigate them?

How has your identity influenced your work as a therapist?

What do you wish you had known at the beginning of your journey that you only learned through experience?

How do you continue developing your skills, professionally, creatively, or personally, after becoming licensed?

What advice would you give to students or early-career clinicians about balancing their own mental health while supporting others?

How do you envision the field of therapy evolving, and what do you think future therapists will need to be prepared for?

What do you wish you had understood earlier about managing finances as a therapist—such as budgeting, setting fees, or navigating private practice income?

How did you learn to handle the tax side of the profession (e.g., quarterly taxes, write-offs, bookkeeping), and what advice would you give to new therapists starting out?

How did you decide whether to work in private practice, a group practice, or community mental health, and what factors most influenced that choice?

Do you currently attend therapy yourself, and how has your own therapeutic work informed your clinical practice?

How did you learn to market yourself as a therapist—whether for private practice, workshops, or community work—and what strategies have been most effective?

SPEAKING TO SUSTAINABILITY

Are you hearing from diverse and inclusive voices? Have you found the folks you wanted to interview who embody the identities and values you hold close? How can you support the person you are interviewing with their goals? Ask for an introduction if it helps you connect with the folks you most want to hear from!

Counseling looks like connection, but it isn't. We hold people's stories without being in their lives, and if we're doing the job well, the boundary is one-way. That's why therapists need community—colleagues who understand the work, and non clinicians who remind us that we're human. Without both, the job warps us. Everything gets too serious, too clinical, too lonely. With the right people around us, though, this work becomes sustainable, meaningful, and deeply fulfilling.

—Tim Wienecke, MA, LPC, LAC

EXERCISE 20

Letter from Your Future Private Practice Self

We are coming close to the end of this workbook! Now it's time to write a letter from your future self as a private practice therapist and business owner to your current self. What would your future self say to you about this process? What words of encouragement would they provide? What messages would they want to convey as they relate to a sustainable and nourishing private practice? Write your letter on the lines below. When you're finished, make two copies of this letter. Keep one somewhere you can return to it. Give the other copy to a trusted person and ask them to mail it back to you one year from the date you write it, as a reminder of who you were becoming and what you knew to be true.

SPEAKING TO SUSTAINABILITY

By keeping your mission in mind, you can do periodic checks of your progress to that end result. Are you in alignment? Are you off track? What can be done next in congruence with your values?

Trust your clinical intuition and know that your therapist parts are wise. Prioritize protecting your energy.

—Crystal Hines, LPC, EMDR Trainer, IFS Consultant, and Founder of Align Therapy and Consultation

You've got this. I am deeply grateful I took the leap to be my own boss and to build up my dream practice. It does require sitting with uncertainty and tolerating the ebbs and flows of pay changes as well as juggling business and therapy hats. It is hard work. And I wouldn't change it for the world.

—SK Wilder, LMFT, she/they

FINAL REFLECTIONS
and Next Steps

What are your hopes, dreams, and aspirations about private practice now? It's been an evolution to go through this workbook and complete every exercise with consciousness and intention.

____

____

How are you feeling about the possibility of private practice now?

____

____

What does social justice have to do with being in private practice. How do you imagine building a private practice that is nourishing and sustainable?

____

____

What are two steps you can take next to be well on your way to launching your therapy business?

____

____

Do what works for YOU!
Know your value.
Set (and maintain) healthy boundaries.
And network, network, network!"

—Shane P. Hodges, LPC w/SPH Counseling (he/him)

THANK YOU!

Consider this workbook an unconventional business plan! After all, it's got your mission, vision, values, and numbers all in one place! Refer back to it regularly to see how things have progressed for you in your business.

If you're willing, we invite you to share your thoughts and feedback by scanning the QR code next to this paragraph. Your reflections will help this workbook grow, change, and evolve over time—so it can continue to be relevant, responsive, and supportive for future therapists.

If we can be of additional support, please don't hesitate to reach out.

Wishing you a fruitful and fulfilling private practice, Sam and Khara